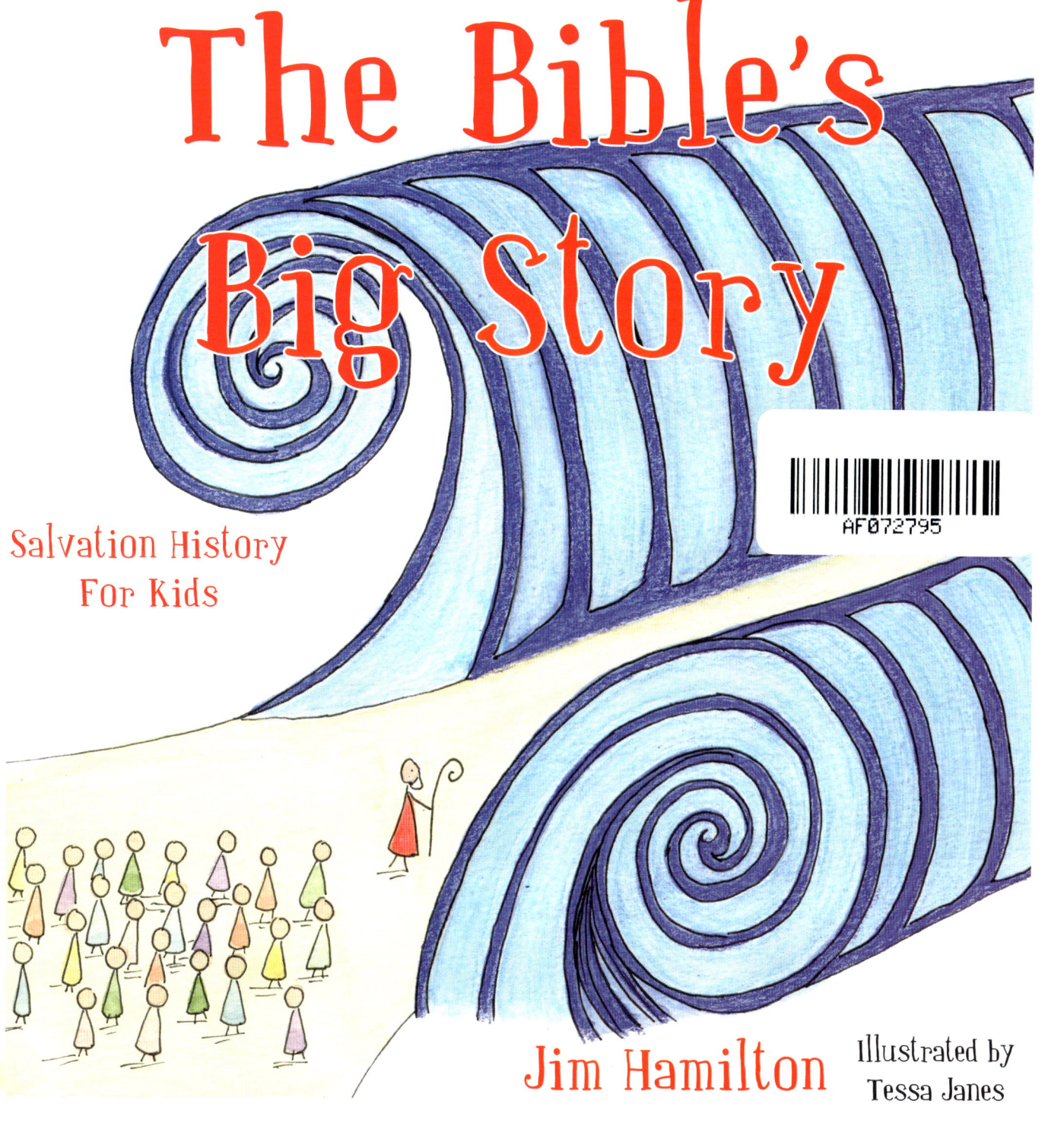

**So, "mother of the living," he named his wife,
For her seed is the source of life.**

The man called his wife's name Eve, because she was the mother of all living.
Genesis 3:20

See also: Genesis 3:21; Genesis 3:23-24.

**Land, seed, and blessing God promised to Abram,
And the nations, also, would be blessed in him.**

'I will make of you a great nation,
and I will bless you and make your name great,
so that you will be a blessing.
I will bless those who bless you,
and him who dishonours you I will curse,
and in you all the families of the earth
shall be blessed.' Genesis 12:2-3

See also: Genesis 15:5-6.

**From Egypt God his people saved,
And at Sinai, the Law he gave.**

The people of Israel went into the midst of the sea on dry ground, the waters being a wall to them on their right hand and on their left. Exodus 14:22

See also: Exodus 20:1-3.

**Then by God's power the land they took,
But then, their good God they forsook.**

So Joshua took the whole land, according to all that the LORD had spoken to Moses. And Joshua gave it for an inheritance to Israel according to their tribal allotments. And the land had rest from war.
Joshua 11:23

See also: Joshua 21:43-45; 1 Samuel 8:7-8.

David's sons forsook the Lord
And did not keep his holy Word.

For when Solomon was old his wives turned away his heart after other gods, and his heart was not wholly true to the LORD his God, as was the heart of David his father. 1 Kings 11:4

See also: 2 Kings 10:32.

The people kept not God's command
And he drove them from the land.

And the LORD said, 'I will remove Judah also out of my sight, as I have removed Israel, and I will cast off this city that I have chosen, Jerusalem, and the house of which I said, My name shall be there.'
2 Kings 23:27

See also: 2 Kings 25:8-11.

Then from exile they returned
And for Messiah they did yearn.

Behold, the days are coming, declares the LORD, when I will raise up for David a righteous Branch, and he shall reign as king and deal wisely, and shall execute justice and righteousness in the land.
Jeremiah 23:5

See also:
Nehemiah 4:6;
Malachi 3:1.

**And so at last God's Son was sent
On an unexpected path he went.**

In the sixth month the angel Gabriel was sent from God to a city of Galilee named Nazareth, to a virgin betrothed to a man whose name was Joseph, of the house of David. And the virgin's name was Mary. Luke 1:26-27

See also: Isaiah 7:14.

**The LORD of all, obedient and humble,
Never did he sin or stumble.**

For we do not have a high priest who is unable to sympathize with our weaknesses, but one who in every respect has been tempted as we are, yet without sin.
Hebrews 4:15

See also: Luke 4:1-2, 13.

**On the cross he paid for sin,
Jesus, Saviour of all men.**

And when they came to the place
that is called The Skull, there they crucified him,
and the criminals, one on his right and one on his left. Luke 23:33

See also: Matthew 21:8-10;
2 Corinthians 5:21;
1 Peter 2:24.

**From the grave he rose again
Conquering death and hell and sin.**

So they went and made the tomb secure
by sealing the stone
and setting a guard.
Matthew 27:66

See also: Matthew 28:2, 4-6.

**To build the church he sent the Spirit.
What good news! All should hear it.**

And divided tongues as of fire appeared to them and rested on each one of them. And they were all filled with the Holy Spirit and began to speak in other tongues as the Spirit gave them utterance. Acts 2:3-4

See also: Matthew 28:18-20.

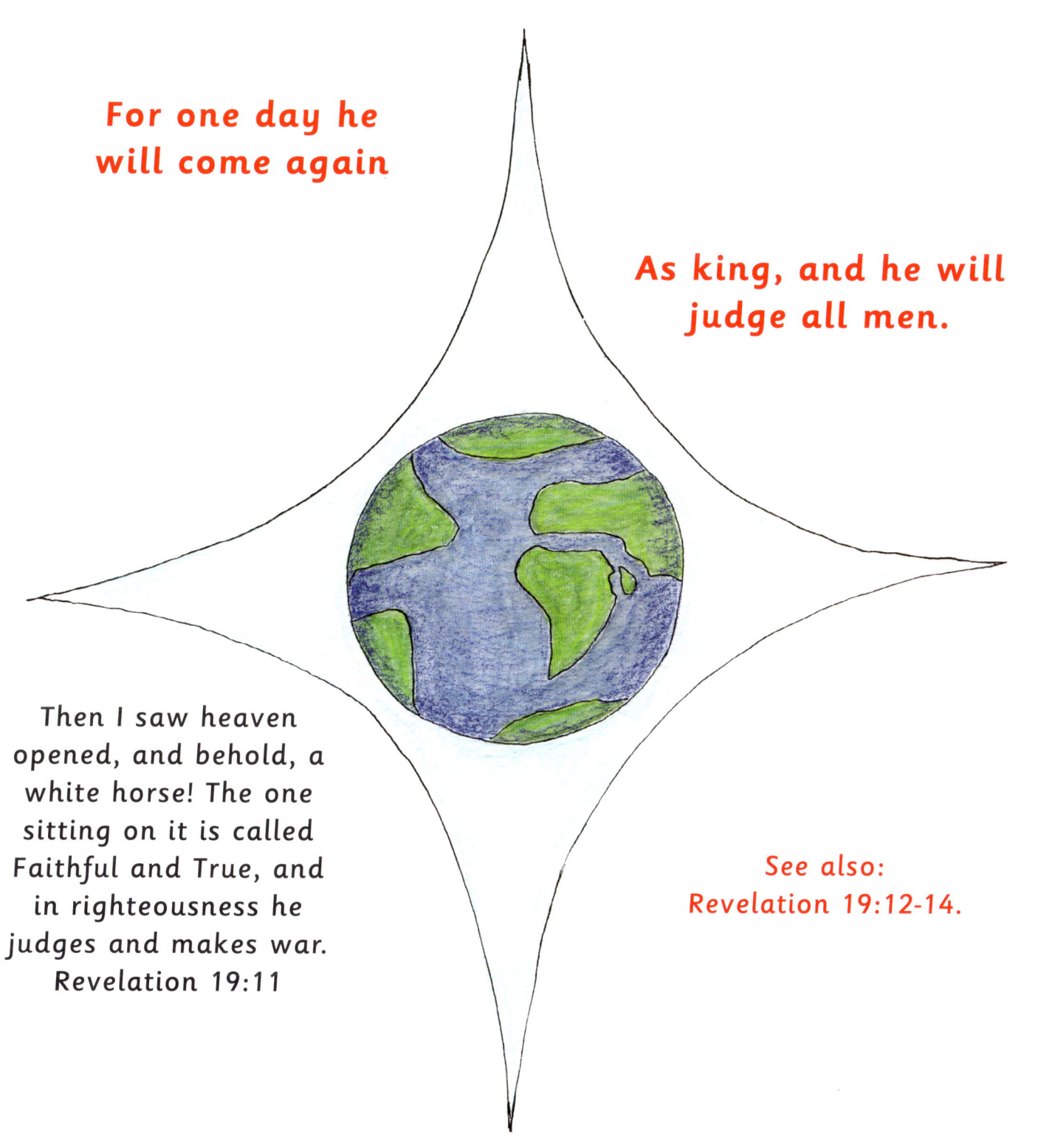

**So let us trust in Christ the Lord
And hold fast to his holy Word.**

Devote yourself to the
public reading of Scripture.
1 Timothy 4:13

See also: 2 Timothy 3:16–4:2;
Acts 20:32; Matthew 16:18; John 17:17.

A Note to Parents

The rhymes of this book seek to capture the big events of the Bible's story. My hope is that knowing these big events will put landmarks in the minds of children and their parents so that they will be able to find their way around and know where they are in the true story of the whole world, the Bible.

The Salvation Historical Timeline

Creation (Genesis 1-2)
Rebellion (Genesis 3)
Promise (Genesis 3:15)
Flood (Genesis 6-9) – Covenant with Noah
Blessing (Genesis 12:1-3) – Covenant with Abraham

The Old Covenant: Preparation

Exodus (Exodus-Deuteronomy) - Covenant with Israel
Conquest (Joshua)
Monarchy (Judges-Kings, 2 Samuel 7) – Covenant with David
Exile (Isaiah-Ezekiel, Hosea-Zephaniah)
Return (Ezra-Nehemiah, Haggai-Malachi)

The New Covenant: Inauguration

Jesus (Gospels)
Cross; Resurrection; Pentecost
Church (Acts, Epistles)

The New Covenant: Consummation

Jesus' Return (Revelation)

May the word of Christ dwell in us richly.
Colossians 3:16

Dedicated to
Gramzee and PawPaw and
Gran and Grandad
Soli Deo Gloria

10 9 8 7 6 5 4 3 2
The Bible's Big Story: Salvation History for Kids
ISBN: 978-1-78191-162-4
Copyright © 2013 James M. Hamilton Jr.
Reprinted 2014
Published by Christian Focus Publications
Geanies House, Fearn, Tain, Ross-shire, IV20 1TW, Scotland, U.K.
www.christianfocus.com
Illustrations by Tessa Janes
Illustrations on this page by the author's son Jake Hamilton when he was 4 years old
All rights reserved. No part of this publication may be reproduced, stored in a retrieval system or transmitted in any form by any means, electronic, mechanical, photocopy, recording or otherwise, without the prior permission of the publisher, except as provided for by USA copyright law.
Scripture quotations are taken from the ESV Bible (The Holy Bible: English Standard Version). Copyright 2001 by Crossway Bibles, a publishing ministry of Good News Publishers. Used by permission. All rights reserved.